THE DOMAIN OF SMALL MERCIES

New & Selected poems (2)
1963 -2016

LOUIS PHILLIPS

Other Works by Louis Phillips

Poetry
Celebrations & Bewilderments (Fragments Press)
Bulkington (Hollow Spring)
The Time, The Hour, The Solitariness of the Place (Livingston Press)
Krazy Kat Rag (Light Imprints)
In the Field of Broken Hearts (Prologue Press)
As Far As I Got (Prologue Press)
R.I.P. (Livingston Press)
The Woman Who Wrote 'King Lear' (Pleasure Boat Studio)
The Kilroy Sonata (World Audience)
American Elegies (World Audience)
Must I Weep for the Dancing Bear? (Pleasure Boat Studio)
The Domain of Silence, The Domain of Absence: New and Selected Poems, 1963-2015 (Pleasure Boat Studio)
The Random Treasury of Best-Loved Poems, editor (Random House)
The Random Treasury of Light Verse, editor (Random House)

Short Story Collections
A Dream of Country Where No One Dare Live (SMU PRESS)
The Bus to the Moon & other stories (Fort Schuyler Press)
The Woman Who Wrote King Lear (Pleasure Boat Studio)
Must I Weep For the Dancing Bear and other stories (Pleasure Boat Studio)
Galahad in the city of Tigers (World Audience Publishers)
Fireworks in Some Particulars –Stories, poems, plays, & humor pieces (Fort Schuyler Press)

Plays
The Last of the Marx Brothers Writers (Broadway Play Publishers)
The Ballroom in St. Patrick's Cathedral (Broadway Play Publishers)

THE DOMAIN OF SMALL MERCIES

New & Selected poems (2)
1963 -2016

LOUIS PHILLIPS

Pleasure Boat Studio: A Literary Press
New York

The Domain of Small Mercies
By Louis Phillips
Copyright © 2017 by Louis Phillips
ISBN 978-0-912887-48-7
Library of Congress Control Number: 2016958704
Design and Cover by Laura Tolkow, laura@flushleft.biz

Pleasure Boat Studio books are available through the following:
SPD (Small Press Distribution)
Partners/West
Baker & Taylor
Ingram Book Company
Brodart
Amazon.com and bn.com

and through

PLEASURE BOAT STUDIO: A LITERARY PRESS

Contact Jack Estes, Publisher
201 West 89th Street
New York, NY 10024

pleasboat@aol.com
www.pleasureboatstudio.com

for

PAT & IAN

and

in memory of Matthew

TABLE OF CONTENTS

POEMS 1963 – 1979

Phillips Has A Falling Out With His Muse	19
Standing At A Gate In Summer	20
& Never Brought To Justice	25
Letters To My Sisters	26
All Send Before Them Into Silence	27
Reflections From La Mancha	28
On Confessional Poetry	30
Dreams We Take To Bed With Us	32
To Those Who Have Wronged Me, Most Unjustly So	34
Metric	36
Morning Song For Pat	37
Nothing In Poetry To Equal It Quite	39
Ordinary Cities	40
Listening To The Sunlight	41
If You Do Not Go Out At Night	42
Love With A Half Life Of 3.92 Seconds	43
Humanities: Three Credits	44
To One Who Suffered A Miscarriage In London	45
Monopoly	47
Love Poem	48
Cinch Strap	49
Between Events	51
Durable	53
A Dance For Big Bad John	54
Make No Bones About It	55
Martian Landscapes	56
Self-Explicating Poem For My Reluctant Readers	57

Interim Report From The City Of Certainties 58
Life Is A Contraption Of Special Effects 59
Living Through History 60
Fatu Hiva 62
67 63
Amid Things Visible 65
Death In The Country 66
Fist 67

POEMS 1980-2012

Reading Poetry Is Not Always The Easiest Thing
    In The World To Do 71
Native American History 72
Barbershop 73
Shadows 74
This Is Just To Say One More Time 76
A Page Untimely Ripped From The Calendar Of
    Earthly Delights 77
The Tent 78
What A Day The Summer Brings 79
One Summer Evening In Connecticut 80
It Escapes Me 81
The Color Of Eyes Of All The Other Characters 82
I Do Not Wish To Live In A World Without Elephants 83
Fire On The Lake 84
Giraffes 85
Aesthetics At 7 A.m 86
Outliving Our Ideals 88
Moving Day 89
Butlers 90
Her Most Human Body 93

The Corridor	94
Outside Of The Hour On The Sea	95
Change Of Scene	96
The Sun Drenched Mornings	97
The Light Is Another Language	98
Everything That Needs To Be Known	99
The Rest Of The World	100
On Reading The Man In The Gray Flannel Suit Some 35 Years After Its Publication	101
Billy Holliday Is Singing & I'm Feeling So Sad	102
Genius To Genius	103
The Circle	104
My Miching Malicho	105
Black Holes In The Galaxy Phillips	106
Perhaps More	107
Roller Coaster Poem	108
The Contours Of Affection	109
It's Not Just Dixie Anymore	110
The Stain	111
Earthquakes	112
Actually	113
The Seasons	114
How Many Lies Must I Tell To Protect Those I Love?	115
Love Poem	116
The Map Of Human Reason	117
The Island	119
The Map Of Human Reason 2	120
Just How Confusing Is Spring	121
Hustling Myself Out Of Existence	122
The Relentless Machinery Of Transport	124
The Structural Linguist Declares His Love To A Woman Named Cadence	125
"The Shining Wings On Which The Dragonfly Rides:"	127

A Man And A Woman Enter The City Of Language
    To Articulate Their Desires 129
Johnny Inkslinger Does The Black Bottom Stomp In Comicstrip
    Land And Rises Up In Disappointment
    In America's Lack Of Values 131
The Creation Of The Gentleman 133
The World It Might Be Said 134
On Reading The Encyclopedia Britannica From
    Cover To Cover 135
All Hell Breaks Loose At This Time Of Year Once Again 136
I Am The Errand Man 137
The Interpretation Of Dreams 138
Blues 140
Happiness 141
A Rain Not Invented By Any Genius 143
Truth Without Embellishment 144
Johnny Inkslinger Presumes To Cut In On Fred Astaire
    While He Was Dancing With Ginger Rogers 145
No Matter What I Do 146
Another Song Of The Cannibals 147
Lacking The Courage To Be Happy 148
For That Summer When All The Wishing Went Out Of Me 149
My Mother The Allegory 150
Crude Night 151
Reading Action Comics 40 Years Too Late 152
The Fury Of Sleet Under Street Lights 153
Adolescence (2) 154
Easter Sunday On The Basketball Court 155
Justice 157
How God Came To Me In Connecticut 159
The Tourniquet 160
The Room 161
April Broadcast 162

Nightwalker 163
Who Would Live In A World Without Singing? 164

NEW POEMS (2013 -2016)
                                                                                        167

It Is 9 A.M. Do You Know Where Your Muse Is? 168
Acceleration 169
Is Poetry A Ticket To Travel 170
Aggiornamento 171
Dawn In A Not So Classical Manner 172
Nothing Miraculous Here 173
Absentee ....
Thinking Of Wallace Stevens On The First   174
    Snowy Day In December 175
Let's Say 176
Further Up The Tracks 178
Lover's Paradox 179
The Rehearsal 180
The Leaping Place Of The Spirit 181
102° In The Shade 182
One Down, 649,000 Hours To Go 183
Sometimes 184
Yorick 186
Hamlet On The Tennis Courts 187
Passing Through The Landscape Will Not Help 188
Worry 189
From One Great Perhaps To Another 190
The Narrows Of Another Life 191
Falling Asleep On The Train To Boston 192
May We Talk About Something Else 193
Ruins ....

There Is Always A Ship Sailing Somewhere
   Over Crazy Weeds 194
Whistling Past The Graveyard In The Better
   Part Of Town 195
Pleasures 196
For My Lost Son 197
Saturday Morning In The Laundry Room 198
Is This What We Have Lived For? 199
American Haiku: The Lie Detector 200
You Could Be Wrong 201
Annual Report From The Planet Money 202
Trouble 101 203
Just Another Spring Poem 204
The Obligatory Scene 205
 All Back Story 206
"Fortune That Arrant Whore" 207
Even Sleep Takes Us Upward 208
Oh God! Not Another Poem About Hope! 209
Field Guide To Wild Flowers 210

POEMS
1963-1979

Phillips Has A Falling Out With His Muse

I've been ordered by my Muse
To fly from London to Sheyang
(Formerly Mukden) & use
My frequent Yang
& Yin of my existence up in the air
Frequent flier miles
Then return the same day
But there's no way
I'm going to do that. I don't care
I'm going to Dodge City instead.

Standing At A Gate In Summer

1.

Nothing holds the sky together
The way a landscape does,
So today the wind scrapes
Upon the hills,
Signaling varieties of weather,
Rising & falling in syllables,
As if there were strength
In holding back,

& thus the weather holds me back.
Certain of rain, I stand at my gate,
Musing on wilderness,
On wild cat, sage, sweetbrier,
Anomalies, & strays. There is
Even adventure in dark places,
Rocks instarred
With rapscallion life,

Miniature moss-lined faces
Of a lapsed world gone underground.
Yesterday I was positive
I could go forth in bad weather,
Entertain with fond grace
The most wild-eyed notions, be a brother
To the Indian & the outcast,
But the mood, if it were a mood,

Has passed…. You see
I need no mountains to cloud my thoughts.

    2.

In Pierre,
They caught Johnny Running Bear,
Relative of Kicking Bear, a Sioux,
& hanged him,

Dangling him
In the afternoon sun.
Reading about him
I recalled the massacre
At Wounded Knee,

200 Sioux --
Men, women & children -- slaughtered
While waiting to surrender.
It was
A simple misunderstanding
The army said.

    3.

I do not idolize the Indians,
That Noble Savage bit
Should have gone by the board
A long time ago, but

I would have a name

Like Running Bear, Little Crow,
Fall From the Clouds, Rain in the Face,
Wolf Robe, Nokoni, Crazy Horse. Now

Those are names to write one's history
With, not like names in my school,
Colorless, pale-face monikers
Recited listlessly from a roll.

    4.

Apache means Enemy.
I shall be the enemy of any man
Who denies these names:

Sioux, Chippewa, Arapaho, Shoshone,
Navaho, Cheyenne, Cree,
Ponca & Kickapoo…Paiute,
Shawnee & Chickasaw & Flathead,
Kiowa, Pueblo, Zuni, Me-Wuk,
Mohave, Yuma, Cherokee, Apache.

    5.

The sun goes sideways,
A pale beetle
In a ghost dance, a ghost dance!

6.

As far as the eye can see,
The wilderness is vanishing,
No Indians, no buffalo,
Merely movie-show

Shoot-outs, covered wagons
Huddled in a rain of arrows,
The Commanche
Painted & whiskeyed,

Spilling under a paramount sun,
Whooping, hollaring
Across the plain,
Threatening John Wayne

& the scrubbed costumed settlers
For the umpteenth time,
The hoop & holler
Of Technicolor.

7.

As I standing at a gate in summer,
The sky, the prairie, the wind itself
Are questions:
    What will grass do?
May grass
Grow taller than a hand.
    What may hand do?
May hand

Grow taller than the eye.
    What must the eye do?
May the eye
Grow tallest of them all

    8.

I grow disconsolate with summer.
I would the warmth were gone,
That wilderness be the weather
In the very mood of land,
For without wilderness
There are no true men.

    9,

Across the field,
 There is the harrow & the plow,
A home to go back to.
I wish to go home.
I wish to be wild.

The wind rushes by
Sucking at its own heels.

    (1972/2016)

& Never Brought To Justice

Hair shaved away, tongues slit,
Flesh fashioned into lampshades,
Or tattooed, bones in a closet –

Such alarms drag me from bed,
My nerves thrown off-balance,
Scrubbed, left to bleed.

One more idiot without sense.
But I write of a girl in Memphis,
Lilting home from a school dance.

Singing what Tennessee has
To offer a black girl in Spring,
April fragrance on the grass.

Atonement is something
Far from her mind, far cry
From her studies, not in her singing,

But when freight trains roll by
In Memphis,
You can't hear a damn thing.

(1966)

Letters To My Sisters

(for Leslie & Lorna)

Though your hearts be huge as April,
They shall, as noiselessly as leaves,
Be broken, & more than once your men
Will leave you, going against their will

& yours to anchor stars above the dead,
To grapple worlds where you will never sit
Nor sleep. More than once, fluid weddings
Of the seasons shall hammer at your beds

Until your hearts break down. But think
Of a city where all the gates have fallen,
Wet streets housed with strangers.
Under a thousand names men eat & drink,

Carry photographs tucked in their sleeves.
Even strangers learn what you soon see:
It is not your fault, nor theirs, necessarily,
That the heart is broken as noiselessly as leaves.

(1963)

All Send Before Them Into Silence

How singular the breath
That changes into sound,
Flute-players' fingers
Poised above the keys,
Sounds that all send,

Before them into silence.
Oh let death be painless
Poised above the keys,
My grandmother nodding

Into sleep, her miraculous
Will let down slowly.
Sitting in the kitchen
Where the light spreads out,
She gathers into Heaven,
If there is a Heaven.

She gathers in the light
Whatever light there is.

(1966)

Reflections From La Mancha

Where madmen ride
Roses are more red
& women pure,

Hearts fall outward
In a lively dance
& need no cure.

If logic need a cell,
The mad go free
To breathe the air,

& whatever life
They crave is theirs
& beyond despair,

Or if windmills turn
Against their lance
Or heated charge,

Or sheep to villains
Or to ogres change
& grow most large,

What matters then
Is knowing how
To break the fall,

Putting cushions down
Beneath the saddle-
Sores & gall...

Against great height
Where dumb-shows play
Their pantomime,

The sane look up
& sprain their necks,
While madmen climb.

(1967)

On Confessional Poetry

No natural thing confesses.
Mole-silent & eye-sore,
Upside-down, the earth is still;
Along any moon-rift shore
Tides cast up a solitary shell,
The long dunes are quiet.
If, in that Pacific roar,
Animal secret finds release,
It is of death or caprice alone.

Muffled by water, by stealth,
Cradled in leaf by stalks
That sonnet & rill,
The smallest orchid tells
No secrets, a small blue mouth
With nothing to say;
Braced to the wind's way,
The tenderest shoot
Casts a redundant shadow.

Still I've heard field mice cry,
Constant threat from above,
Owl wing fluttering
When I was helpless to save
Its victim, to save anything
From itself & its own escape.
In that predatory swoop,
Moons & meadows
Wrinkled spines in a hush.

No natural thing tells all.
For what is at the lips
Is the nerves' slow progress,
Sun's battering, slip
Of the throat in distress.
I would tell all I could
About myself, if I did not know it
As a way of covering my tracks
When the wind was on me & the rain.

(1969)

Dreams We Take To Bed With Us

Sometimes they are of greatness—
Napoleon in his hat,
His hand within his coat —
Or of such monument that careless
    Gestures spell an end
    To empires & to friends.

Sometimes the outstretched hand
Heals the sick, begs the lame
To walk, or greets
Old loves, women who sit
Right down on us & have no shame,
    A concert of sighs,
    Legs & thighs.

Sometimes we dream of death,
Black wagons in the road,
The hearse gleaming, horses
Pulling at halter as
The corpse is unloaded,
    Symbolic funeral
    Of the real & unreal.

Our days' events are spelled
Out in dreams we take to bed
With us, the good, the bad,
The merely indifferent. I said
I would dream of you & be glad,

Would sail past sleep
With you, yet keep

You by my side. I said I would
Always make a dream meadow
For you to lie in, summers
Of wind blossom, when air
Refused to drop like a petal.
I said I would always sail
  Past sleep with you,
   & I do. Sometimes....

(1969)

To Those Who Have Wronged Me, Most Unjustly So

Biologists, philosophers,
Even our Savior
Have often sought keys
To human behavior,

Now the secret I've hit on
Makes moralists cringe,
But I speak it out loud:
We want revenge,

& the successful evolution
Of humankind
Is based on the art
Of hitting from behind.

I say it in whimsy,
I write it in black:
Whatever wrong is done to us
We do back.

Christians may mutter
From now to next week
The stunning virtue
Of turning one's cheek,

But the truth of the matter
Of where Life is at
Is – this is the universe
Of tit for tat,

Or if I may muster
My bedroom wit,
Love's the refreshing exchange
Of tit for tit.

Thus, this is my slogan,
So humanly true:
If you screw me,
I screw you.

(1969)

Metric

No one knows this cadence
As well as I.
I measure it
Beneath your eye,

Stop. Pause,
& then run on.
A cadence is
A falling down.

To keep a cadence
One must let
A line go slack,
Loosen up a bit

To keep a rhythmic
Phrase
From falling in,
& out of phase.

Whether or not
This poem is true,
You go the way
I tell you to.

(1972)

Morning Song For Pat

Sleep now.
There will be no more bad dreams.
If nightmares come,
I shall ward them off with an umbrella,
Feinting & lunging,
Saying, "Take that! Bad dreams be gone!"

Shhh! Take
To sleep as you would glide through water
Slowly. It's all right.
Don't clench your fists so tightly,
Thrashing your head
Upon the pillow, crying, "No, No, Not me!

Be gone!"
With names I cannot decipher.
If nightmares come,
I shall cover our wood floor with tacks.
The crooked dreams will hop about,
Holding their feet & shouting, "I'll

Be damned
If I visit such a crazy broad again."
Starched chickens search for their heads,
A subway is crowded with knives.
Windows bleed. *Shhh!* now.
Everybody has them. It's all right. I'll

Put hamburgers
In the kitchen. If Evil hungers for you
He'll eat my cooking & die.
There is nothing in this room to harm you.
Nightmares prefer air-conditioning.
It's all right. Everything's all right.
Sleep now.

(1970)

Nothing In Poetry To Equal It Quite

No synonym for wind,
Sweet gale swaying high branches full of juice,
Nothing in poetry to equal it quite.
Ferreting daylight
Overlaps with my life & unsorry
With so much bright boasting & souse.
With phosphoreted green wings
Offspringing in noon-light.
A glimpse: the white-rumped Harrier
Chu-chu-chu. Chu-chu-chu.
What does it matter
My hand to this world? My face?
The sun may shoal out of this quickening
For l00,000,000 yrs. or so. & then?
But, right at this moment,
My path to the world's heart
Thickens, then brightens, then thickens.

(1975)

Ordinary Cities

Geography to the last,
Dead rivers to cross,
Full budget
Of abandoned mines,
Capitals with black stars,
Cities written in red
To differentiate them
From the ordinary.
The Nile is one blue line,
As is the Amazon
& all rivers where
Natives
With foreign breasts
Leap holus-bolus.
At last in this Atlas
The yellow spine
Of deserts, quarries,
Ink-blot lakes, stem
Of side roads
Without numbers,
Boundaries all.
So many inches to the mile
We crawl
Going nowhere,
Returning with hope.
Maps!
Bring me more maps.
Let me see
Where I am going.

(1979)

Listening To Sunlight

Slowly my morning opens
To arpeggios in tangents.
Alternate melodies
Edging from rooftops
To forests to allegro
Pink on the windows
Somewhat with full voice
One fling of *fa*
Into the Long River,
Repeated chords,
Waves in triplets,
Then a half step down,
Deeper into spacious
Curious scales,
Blue hills beyond
Awaiting percussion,
Sharp triads &
Now the first
Movement has ended.

(1979)

If You Do Not Go Out At Night

If you do not go out at night,
You soon forget how dark country roads get.
My wife & I are driving
From small town to small town &
God has invented new ways to die.
Young animals break from the brush,
Then freeze in the headlight, &
No other traffic holds the road.
No one behind us, &
No one coming toward us &
A light rain falling.
The scraping of windshield wipers
Creates a dense & private music.
All the way on our brights,
Until I begin to wonder:
Suppose we are no longer alive,
Is this what Eternity is really like:
An endless road winding about
Lakes & houses we cannot see,
Terrified creatures gibbering in panic?

(1975)

Love, With A Half-Life Of 3.92 Seconds

Tormented with heat
Over melancholy bodyscape,
Lava's hard core,
Like hey-go-mad,
No languishing here.
Gone fission.
What will wags say?
Half-life is better
Than no life at all? Escape!
Puritan lawmakers warn:
Do not undress in public.
No lying down. No? Yes?
Under such rebuke.
O love, under your skirts,
Creased, no anti-matter,
My hands go mad. Pubic
Hadrons, atomic mime,
When fuck-mood
Takes you to its arms,
Here is the join.
Where nucleons collide,
Midnight floods the field.
With more charm than
The 4th quark. What ho!
Unembellished electrons work.
The outside world is larger than us,
But we pay it no heed,
Because flesh has
A life of its own. Yes? No? *(1972)*

Humanities: Three Credits

Far from the Ungererstrasse,
My students gaze upon me with pity.
I am the daft man
Trying to hoist Odysseus from the dead,
10th round of *The Trojan Women*,
Euripides in pink hair, tragic earrings.
Upon the screen,
Women in black
Wander & wail. Grief without suspense.
For some, grief is a high wall,
Many-towered,
Built by Apollo & Poseidon.
For others, it is a city
Where one's family lives
With friends. Outside the wind is blowing.
For my students,
Half-asleep with boredom,
Grief is a ship with sails,
Or a faraway port
No one visits.

(1972)

To One Who Suffered A Miscarriage In London

It is summer in Dublin,
With tourists guidebooking
The soil, hiking up to farms,
Castles, towers, & ruins,
Then turning to London, looking

For antiques, buckramed books,
Prints of Daunty, Gouty,
& Shopkeeper, following a bridge
That falls down, pleasant leas,
A fat wind to squeeze

Into the Holy Pews. No one
Ever thinks of loss. After all,
Who gets sick in London?
Only the natives. Once in a while
A cat. It must be a miserable

Time to get sick in, no friends
Around, & the sights bending
A finger, saying, "Come here!"
It shows you cannot depend
On journeys to save you, nor literature

Nor pregnancy, nor husbands,
Nor houses. What do men
Of breeding do
With loss, with pain? Screw
Us all. We make books & pretend

45

To be a sensitive lot. We
Existentialize on the Absurd.
Good God, woman! You are
Ill in London & in Dublin
& I offer you these useless words.

(1969)

Monopoly

Hand-coupling
Should have been obsolete
& it was, but it cost money
To install
New devices,
So Frank Evans lost both legs
In Baltimore,

Crushed
Between trains, was "retired"
Without a pension.
That same year
Frederick Vanderbilt,
Grandson of the Commodore,
Completed an estate,

$660,000
Worth of home, unfurnished.
The rich are great
Philanthropists.
They give until it hurts.

(1971)

Love Poem

Late night,
Cries of an anguished animal
Escape from my body,
A wounded animal
With its neck broken,
Mourning dove cooing,
Fox bleeding at mouth,
Wolf gnawing at its own leg to get free.
Love, place your head
Upon my chest.
Listen.

(1971)

Cinch Trap

The cinch strap,
Tight across the loins,
Makes the horse buck.
When he feels
A buckle by his rump,
He knows it is no game.
His aim
& the rider's aim
Are not the same.

The chute leaves
Little room to maneuver in.
White slats
Hedge him in on all sides,
Along with a man
Who hits him across the face
With a rope
To make him behave.
The rider adjusts his glove,

Then sits down gently,
Barely grazing the saddle,
His right arm high in the air.
The gate opens, rather
Is opened, the sweating horse
Bolts forward, head down,
Spinning back toward the fence,
Always its head low on the chance

That the rider will fall
Head over head,
Then he'll step on his face &
Break the rider's jawbone.
After the 10 second buzzer,
The rider is pulled free,
The cinch strap untied,
The horse herded to a pen.
Then the next chute opens.

(1972)

Between Events

At the outdoor rodeo
In Davy,
My father perched
On a slat fence
That rimmed the top of the grandstand.
At that distance
He could barely see
The Brahmas bob & weave,
Tornadoes of dust
At the clowns' shanks,
Or shimmering rope
Over the calves' necks.
My own neck was sweat & dirt
Partially hidden
By a red bandanna.

Between events,
I glanced back thru the crowd,
Watching the white shirt
Balancing on a fence,
Worried that my old man
Might topple backward
Into the parking lot
40 feet below,
But that's how it is
When you're somebody's son.
The men on the bucking horses
Slammed out of the chutes,
Round eyes riveted to blur,

Their legs flapping.
In an earlier event,
Number 4
Had broken his back,
But we all have somebody else
To worry about.

(1972)

Durable

Majestic with buzz,
Late summer retakes the field. Operatic heartbeats
In full swing,
Ersatz growls of hope & despair.
Another summer, another Winter.
If you live long enough,
The phrase "Everything is lost"
Becomes a sledge hammer to the heart.
Beyond the hedgerows & fields,
One more decaying house
On a block of decaying houses.
My mother, on her wedding day,
Received a large cedar chest
That followed her from house to house.
My sisters and I wd open the chest
To marvel at the smell,
Fragrance so thick
You cd cup it in your hands,
Transfixed in a room so tiny
We could barely turn around.

(1978)

A Dance For Big Bad John

For the poet John Logan

If there is a God in heaven,
Let us
Dance in the streets
With madcap whirling,
Until sleepers awake &
Walk downstairs,
Their dreams in their hands,
Saying, "Take them, take them,
You have awakened us with music."

(1975)

Make No Bones About It

Our Worlds spin,
Tongues wag.
How easily we are whisked
Out of existence
With gossip & friskings

But, with us or without us,
Make no bones about it,
Spring will be at it again
With flossflowers & moles
Crashing & splicing

From one end of the field
To another. Hint of mist
Over & under soil,
Swift, soft splinters
Of rain. How we flail

At Life's spells, precise
Mellow witchcraft
Under the blank stare
Of a moon
That sees nothing,

(1979)

Martian Landscapes

O red sacrarium to War &
Husbanding mutants,
Sweet/sour cats bulging with Krypton &
Myriad scorched substances,
Don't let Science
With its big cameras do you in.

Ready to knuckle under
To your gynecocracy,
I am in my rocket now.
Hold back your parvoline,
Your hydrogen,
Your Death-Rays like big boobs.
Hells bells,
The runes of age are on me.
Earth is a canal of bloat,
All hype & shit.
I desire something more dangerous,
More fantastic.
I lust for diaphanous skulls,
Babbling-indecent-
Cuneiformed-multi-breasted virgins,
Strontium tongues down my throat.
I desire multifid monsters
To commit sodomy upon.
O grant me a Thulium ear to kiss!

(1979)

Self- Explicating Poem For My Reluctant Readers

Find the lines in this poem that show:
The reader is not hostile to the author,
That Antony in power
Is as headstrong as Caesar was,
That God is fundamentally superstitious &
Will not light 3 universes upon a single match,
That Pompey had been as popular as Caesar,
That these words are obeyed without question,
That the conspirators regard with contempt
The sea that surrounds Caesar,
That certain critics regard with contempt
Anything that is not theirs,
That the addition of a foreign language
"Es preciso matar al rubio vendedor de aguardiente..."
Makes the hearts of professors seeking tenure
Leap for joy! Finally, referring to line 2,
Show how each reader
Turns upon the conspirators &
Drives them from the city, onto the beach
Where the ocean gives everyone full credit &
The Milky Way is repeated in the nodding of a head,
The winking of an eye, the lifting of a hand.
We have so many questions to answer,
But History only pretends to be friends to conspirators.
Who are the conspirators?
Why you and I, of course.
Didn't you know? I thought you knew.

Interim Report From The City Of Certainties

There is certain pleasure in being precise,
But I who have lived so long amid rumors,
Reverse blend shirtings of automated advice,
Frequently believe I shall speak to someone
& be understood. *E.g..* What Richard Nixon
Is reputed to have said: "I know that you believe
You understand what you think I said,
But I'm not sure you realize
That what you heard is not what I mean." Or,
"The entities of which one is talking
Must be taken out of their hiddenness;
One must let them be seen as something unhidden."
My loyalty is yours for the asking,
If you only know how to ask right.
Anyway, you know what I mean.

(1978)

Life Is A Contraption Of Special Effects

Isn't it odd how Life, being a series of temporary reprieves,
Is a contraption of special effects?
Cecil B. de Mille, not God, parted the Red Sea.
I thought of that this morning
When a red-winged blackbird flew to the feeder.
Just because something is foolish
Does not mean it is not true: *e.g.*
You start out to be God or Tolstoi
Or some person with a superior soul, &
You become someone you never planned to be,
Become nobody but yourself. How sad.
It's only Life that keeps me from my life,
If you know what I mean.

(1978)

Living Through History

For 444 days, Americans
Were held hostage in Iran.
How easily my own life
Went on. My wife & I
Made love as if there were
No hostages, children
Ran home from school, &,
As if there were no hostages,
Ice-cream trucks played
Their melodic soft wares.
8 Americans
Died in the desert,
Crewmen burned alive
In an aborted rescue mission
Involving helicopters &
Desperation. In the movies,
As if there were no hostages,
Dirty Ducks went
To their deaths &
Villains opened & closed
Warehouses of special effects.
I wound my watch
As if there were no hostages,
Laced my shoes,
Worried about money. In 1979,
Blindfolded Americans
Were paraded
Thru the streets of Teheran.
Other persons suffer,

But their pain
Is not our pain.
We do not feel it
With the same intensity.
This we call
Living thru History.

    (1979)

Fatu Hiva

"Renowned, according to a Norwegian encyclopedia, 'for cannibalism and fornication.'"

Alas! My ambitions are too low.
I shd be remembered for
Cannibalism & fornication.
Phillips? Ah, yes. Devoured
The population of Bel Harbor!

Fornication? Don't say it!
Too disgusting to consider.
Banned from Boston & New Hebrides.
Phillips? Ah, yes. The Fatu Hiva
Of the *dummity dum dum* set,
Raging to the gills. Anger. *Grrr.*

According to his brides,
His heart a Chinese acrobat,
Thumpety-thumping contorted,
Distorted & all that jive.
Phillips? His world is fat.
With Envy, that old dog
Who lies down with him,
Sleeps by his side & growls.
  Phillips? His Being howls
For what he does not understand,
Tho his memory shim-
mers with all he loves....
All those he loves,
He devours alive.

(1979)

67

I should like to live
Until I was 67,
At least 67.

Quasimodo lived to 67,
& Robert Bridges
Lived

What must have seemed
Forever,
Aches for every year,

& all of us know
Someone
Who died too young.

But 67
Has dignity,
Time to leap from a hotel bed,

Crotchety, cantankerous,
Calling the manager,
Flustering

The maid, saying
"Goddamn it!
I'm 67 years old &

I've worked hard
For my money.
How about a little service

In this hotel?"

    (1970)

Amid Things Visible

> *"I experience an immense need for happiness, and I find no way to satisfy it amid things visible."* Paul Claudel

Is there anything better
Than to bicycle around the lake?
Oh sure. There is
Superstar-hit-the-mirrored-
Ceiling-put-it-anywhere
Sex, but with Hermes
On my handlebars,
Grant me this July
With cowhead sunshine
Mooing its moo
Over obstacles of flesh.
Did not Titania
Whisper in my ear
"Thou art as wise
as thou art beautiful"?

Deciding on new ways to die,
Boozy fishermen on the bridge
Dangle night-crawlers,
Then spit, then wave,
Though from where I sit
I see dolphins rise &
Showy Lady's Slippers bow
As I ride by. O God
I am so happy.
What is wrong with me?

(1977)

Death In The Country

Here in the country
You either feed
Run-away animals
Or not. It's a principle of sorts.
From the open field
A scrawny cat sobs, childlike,
To break my heart.
Will I live long enough
To see deer run to my front porch?
I push open the screen door
& walk outside,
Placing my arms around the neck
Of a 12-point buck,
Hugging him,
His melancholy face
Against my face
& no one dies ever.

(1974)

Fist
———

We climb out of the world
Hand over fist,
The rope, our being,
The fist, our hearts.

    (1974)

POEMS

1980 - 2012

Reading Poetry Is Not Always The Easiest Thing In The World To Do

If you are reading this poem
While running away
From 3 or 4 Russian spies
Who have silencers
On their guns
& umbrellas with poisoned tips,
You are, most likely,
Not giving this poem
The full attention it deserves.

(2012)

Native American History

What do I know
But that we come & go.
Come & go, I said,
Thru whiplashes of summer
With its seasonal rumors,
Thru visible violence
We call History. I saw once
The upper meadow
Crowded
With 110 Crow dead.

(2011)

Barbershop

Samson among the Philistines,
I began every school year with a haircut.
"Get your hair cut," my father
Sd & so I did. But

My first week at college, six years
After the Supreme Court ruled
"Separate educational facilities are
Unequal," my barber railed.

(In Florida. I had asked for a trim.)
Pressing hard his straight razor
Against my Adam's apple,
Asked: "How do you feel about them

Letting niggers into our schools?"

(2006)

Shadows
───────

Poplars, beeches, & birches,
Like soldiers
Snapping to attention,
Stand straight up.

The gallows at Theresienstadt
Were built high enough
So that Jews being executed
Cd see a patch of the world
As it was being pulled out
From under them.

Throughout death camps,
In the shadows of ruined buildings
Shameless beauty
Has spring up,
Not exactly overnight. Grass

Cd not be more green,
Potato fields lush with flowers.
Further off, sounds of a river
Running straight & true.
Nature cannot be more giving.

Eons before Facebook,
My parents sat by the radio,
War news & Lamont Cranston.
The Shadow asked:
"Who knows what Evil
Lurks in the hearts of men?"

The answer, of course:
The survivors do.

    (2011)

This Is Just To Say One More Time

I have read
about plums
that were in
the icebox

that poem
the professor
was saving
for a final exam

Forgive me
the poem was
so sweet
and so short

(2010)

A Page Ripped Untimely
From The Calendar Of Earthly Delights
───────────────────────────────

When I fall in love with a woman
Who possesses a Latin face, noble carriage, or a figure
Promising on the calendar of earthly delights --
A new holiday! One in red letters!

I soon discover, unlike Columbus or Casanova,
She is completely up-to-date,
Contemporaneous with the next century,
Complete with rocket boosters,

Whereas I am wandering, perplexed & lost,
In Late Medieval and Renaissance Europe.

    (2011)

The Tent

When I am sad,
My life folds up inside of me
Like a small tent

Which I carry
To the ends of the earth,
Where, as the universe

Drifts & shifts after dark,
I lie down under a net of stars
Whose weight

Is nearly as great as my own.

(2012)

What A Day In Summer Brings

Flowing water allows the universe
To be my handmaiden.
As I speak my innermost thoughts,
A dragonfly sits upon my chest,
Sunlight shining thru its wings,
As if I am nothing but a rock.

(2001)

One Summer Evening In Connecticut

By 8 P.M. the evening is sweet roasted
With pine, mint, raccoon, & wind,
Each mingles with equal ease,
While my sons,
Erratic with heartache
Run from bedroom to living room,
Then back again,
Shouting at the top of their lungs
"John Quincy Adams! John Quincy Adams!"
Lackaday! How do you figure it?

(1990)

It Escapes Me

How they smuggled a coil of rope into my cell,
Procured a hacksaw & a gun,
Not one of the prisoners is squealing,
But on Friday last,
2 dangerous truths escaped from me.
Sirens, bells, whistles, all manner of alarm.
½ hour later the sheriff
Produced, as if out of thin air,
3 scrawny bloodhounds, 2 ex-cons,
& one flat-bottomed boat
For entering the swamp
Where the saw grass grows. 3 days later
We emerged smelling of old tires.

There must be an island somewhere
That humankind has overlooked.
We were, as you can well imagine,
No wiser than before.

    (2006)

The Color Of Eyes Of All The Other Characters

I never was much on this book reading, for it takes 'em too long to describe the color of the eyes of all the characters.
 Will Rogers

With wind & fog &
Like a kelpie in the well,
Her eyes are dark
As days gone round, filled
With grey & wonder,
Like Latin for a world
Where all other languages
Are forgotten, hymns
Obscurely sung
For the goddess Hecate.
Jesus! Where did you get
Those peepers?

   (2010)

I Do Not Wish To Live In A World Without Elephants

Frequently our dreams are not mammoth enough.
It is mealy, this world with so little substance.
No. No more poetry! I shall say it bluntly:
I do not wish to live in a world without elephants.
Wide-eyed I listen for the click of tusks,
Herds of elephants rumbling into the bush.
By way of greeting, elephants place their trunks
Into one another's mouths. How shall my sons grow
Without sensing the imponderable bulk of the world?
Elephants, like us, have been known to die of grief.
How necessary it is, even in so paltry a landscape,
Ivory-stained, & large enough only for killing,
To be reminded of life larger than ourselves.
More than 50,000 muscles in the trunk alone, &
Then it happens: a large orange moon trumpets
Over the woodland; suddenly we sense a planet going musth.

(1980)

Fire On The Lake

How incoherent all our lives are.
Standing in the rain, I think:
The lake resembles,
Cloudy, moody,
The back of a hand burnt by fire,
Until the wind
Unsettles it, relinquishing stars.

(1981)

Giraffes

My brain is no farther from my body than she is.
We giraffes seemingly so frail,
Have this in common:
The distance from brain to heart.
If we fall down, we can't get up.

(2000)

Aesthetics At 7 A.m.

We judge others
By standards
Higher than ones
We use upon ourselves,
But how does one know the weather
Unless one is out in it?
This morning
The sleet sleets &
One small hawk
Poses amid white-flaked branches
For its portrait (cubist).
I have been reviewing
Amid "shivering owls souse"
A book about Picasso
When my 3 yr. old son calls,
"Daddy, throw Bunny downstairs!"
45 years old &
I spend most of my waking hours
Searching for stuffed animals.
Isn't it time I painted from life?
I locate Bunny
Behind the sofa,
Walk to the top of the narrow
13-step stairwell
To give a high toss.
The animal arcs purely,
High, magnificent,
Lands square on target,
Right on my son's outstretched arms.

"Good throw, Daddy!"
Good catch, I tell him.
Positive reinforcement
All the way down the line.
Deep in his blue period,
My son's pajama-clad body
Turns the corner,
Scampers out of sight.
The arc, the child, the catch:
How dare Picasso's "Three Graces"
Compete with any of these?
I turn toward the window,
Sleet has stopped,
The hawk has flown,
Purely, surely magnificent,
Real life.
The Buddha's Four Truths
Fall upon my soul in a heap.
I too have turned a corner.
There is now no retreat.

(1992)

Outliving Our Ideals

Bad music is playing, &
Like many another
I am waltzing toward loss
With its small potatoes.
Of course, I had ideals
But now I am well aware
Of the strain & toss
Of Luck & Fate,
How brutal God's
Indifference is,
How dazzling is
My fall from grace,
How sudden, how final.
Yet my spirit waltzes
To the "possibilities of things."

(2010)

Moving Day

I have been weeping.
Tears from mouth even,
For it is moving day.
I am packing it in.
Love. Too big. Can't fit
In the van, &
Slightly smaller crates
For Forgiveness, Sadness,
Entire rooms of moods.
No need to mark the boxes
With X's, they shall arrive
At their proper destination
Without any help
On my part. As for Rage,
There is no carton
Large enough.

(2010)

Butlers

Rhett was no butler,
Nor am I,
But I am enthralled
By

Movies that show butlers
Bustling & butlering
Within huge mansions
Thronged

With mirrored hallways,
Intoxicated guests,
Evening-gowned dowagers
With busts

Slightly larger than Rhode Island,
Men in tuxedos --
All with splendid manners,
Knowing do's

& don'ts of silverware,
How to close a deal,
Or select French wine.
How real,

How very real
The rich are; their children
Have at least 4 names
& depend

Upon nannies or maids
To give them
Anything they want
To satisfy their every whim.

The ordinary world
Is raw
With Danger, so we
Beg to fight their wars,

Grind their steel,
Obey their laws, worship inheritance.
Within their iron gates,
I do my song & dance,

Thinking of my old man,
His money worries,
His ulcers churning overtime,
His need to curry

With the Boss.
A roof over our heads,
Food on the table --
Whatever we had

Cost more than we cd afford.
Every appliance, every car
Secondhand.
But we were workers,

Hard workers with Greek pride
& Irish pleasures,
Yet, no matter how hard we tried,
Rest assured,

We never wd be as real
As those others,
Those shadows in well-lit movies,
Waited on by butlers.

(2012)

Her Most Human Body

When she do not say "Stop!"
Her most human body
One hop on the A Train,

& her cherry heart a popsicle
Ripe for melting. Here we go
A summer treat!

Hells bells her breasts. Sweet
Are the uses thereof. How quickly
In & out of tune my sinuses

& free trade. How diverse
Her enchanting esplanade
Of pleasures. How did I come here

Cherished & writhing?

(1981)

The Corridor

The corridor of old age:
What a long solitary walk
From one end to the other.
I had almost forgotten
How sweet the world cd be
Until I stopped at my bedroom door
To observe my wife sleeping.
The briefest moment of joy
Knowing that, for a few hours,
She wd be free from pain.

(2012)

Outside Of This Hour On The Sea

Outside of this hour on the sea.
We imagine the Antipodes
Where the sun rises at midnight
&, as Theocritus sd,
"In sleep, every dog dreams of food."
But when I dream,
I am wandering in a house
Near the ocean
Where the waves are black & high.
It is my house & not my house,
& persons inside are quarreling
Because I am late, or early, or lost.
Inside this house,
There is always a room
I have never known about,
Did not know it existed.
A door opens. Inside is a woman.
She stands with her arms
Folded across her chest,
A sign of modesty or diffidence.
"Enter," she says. "Enter."
Through a window, the sea surges.
Breaking waves seem to ask:
Why are you here? Where are you?
Outside of this hour on the sea,
Who are you really?

(2011)

Change Of Scene

What is best for a world that shimmers?
What I need is a change of scene,
To look thru clean windows for a change,
To sleep in a strange bed,
But the days sit on me like a bruise.
The upstairs clock chimes like Britain.
4 days I have searched for
The plumage of a foreign bird!
But all I see is one tiny cardinal,
Setting its keen throat
(With its black dicky)
On a naked branch. I watched it remain
Motionless for hours,
But when I fetched my sons to look,
To share the scene with me,
The cardinal had flown. I took that to be a sign,
A sign to change my life.
Instead, I turned on the radio.
No matter where I am,
The news is very much the same.

(2011)

The Sun Drenched Mornings

I must not lay upon my children
The full burden of my heart --
They have their own lives to lead.
They think about beginnings,
I concentrate upon endings.
If the sundrenched mornings
Are too cold for comfort,
Who am I to warn them?

(1992)

The Light Is Another Language

I have nothing up my sleeve.
In fact, I do not have a sleeve.
This poem conceals nothing,
Has nothing to hide,
Every word is out in the open
Where it can be seen,
Can be seen because light itself
Is another language.

(2009)

Everything That Needs To Be Known.

I look out the window to see
A field of wild daisies upon
Which sunlight flames, &
Purple plants without names
Known to me.
In that instant silently framed
Everything I am
Rises out of my soul, &
I know everything that needs to be
Known. It passes.
I step off the bus
Into real estate & groceries.

(2008)

The Rest Of The World

As I wander in & out of curio shops,
No one notices. But a woman in my building
Has so many children
I never see her on the street
Without at least one daughter in tow,

But on Liuichang Street,
On another continent,
What shall we think of Hu Lijiao
Who was once a member of the "Little Devils"
& took part in The Long March?

Afterwards, the peasants in Linyi County
In Shanxi Province raise their heads
& ask for food.

Far from China is Brazil
Where the Archbishop Camara sd:
"When I give food to the poor,
They call me a saint.
When I ask why the poor
Have no food,
They call me a communist."

Ah! The rest of the world!

(2005)

On Reading The Man In The Gray Flannel Suit *Some 35 Years After Its Publication*

The ironclad silences of Greentree Avenue.
Somewhere in the back of our minds is something less involved,
For when we move this far out from the city,
We soon know what we are going to become.
Mortgages get ripe this time of the year &
Erratic moonlight spins over cinnamon stones,
So much of what we were is foreclosed
Before we have even gotten started.
"Life isn't worth living like this."
Train stations impacted like microfilm,
Kitchen kisses, moving-out parties, school taxes,
Reflex of crooked fears over the Merritt Parkway.
Can Westport be the center of the world forever?
"It's just that nothing seems to be fun anymore."
We glance out our windows and think:
Ours is the kind of life anyone can satirize,
But it is who we are, conspirators
Plotting against our own best interests.
Chapter 24: "The important thing is to make money."
Indian summer & the trees are ensnarled
With sunlight making its own long commute.

(2010)

Billie Holiday Is Singing & I'm Feeling So Sad

Good morning, heartache.
Oh don't tell me what kind
Of a dog-assed day it's going to be.
Let me find out for myself.
Here comes a long clarinet solo,
Sex without foreplay.
Let's knock the bitch around a little longer.
Take a quick look at the bed
& head for another town.

Hardship is one kind of music,
Flump of the feds sitting on her head
Because she ain't
Completely hobbled by cocaine yet.
The world with its hot rods
Of whoring & waiting
Is smarter than anyone knows,
No matter what is sad,

No matter what is sd
Nor how it is sd,
No matter how much hardship,
How much pain struggles
Into her throat.
Hardship is the music.
Give the piano player a drink, &
Shake it for all you is worth.

Billie Holiday is singing
  && I'm feeling so sad.   *(2009)*

Genius To Genius

One of those weeks of high humidity
When you stand
In the apse of the Church of S. Clemente,
Dripping with masterpieces & sweat,
Feeling that perhaps this wd be
The perfect time
To have a heart to heart
With Federico Fellini, mentor
To distorted faces,
Small-town tragic lives,
Masterpieces of the Catalan School, or
Discuss the meaning of life, war,
Love, circuses, peacocks in snow,
Until the Maestro stares at me
As if I were mad.
After all, I don't even speak Italian.

(2007)

The Circle

It is difficult,
Amid frequent shifting
Of Time & the Self

To walk around
Your own life.
With every step

The Circle grows larger.
Even the Dead
Sit inside it.

More steps, more Time,
More selves.
The Circle remains unmoved.

(2011)

My Miching Malicho

We touch the world any way we can.
It stinks with touches.
Hags of midnight sleep
With all the furies,
Roots, bones, & old loves.
How does one escape
The song of stench, its lively air?
Lizards turn
To colors of their tongues.
No need to reach out,
The world comes at its own good pace.
Call it love,
Call it what you will,
We make a terror of ourselves.
Not all the skin in the world
Will help us here.

(1999)

Black Holes In The Galaxy Phillips

falls into deep gravity,
Say the gravity of some 10,000,000 suns.
The 200 inch telescope at Palomar
Has observed
Something that has never happened,
Tho it will happen again. A collapsed star
Forming the heart of
Whatever it is he lost.
Aquila non captat muscas,
But flies come buzzing all day long, &
Who is to say who is an eagle?
Radiant energy lost,
Siphoned off,
Matter packed so densely
That not even light
Can escape its pull.
He asks: What shall I do with my life?
The answer is shipped to him from afar:
You did it.

(1999)

Perhaps More
_____

The husband of my neighbor
Has been dead for 15 years.
Perhaps more.

Someday, some young person,
Slouching against a wall.
Will make

Similar remarks about myself:
"He has been dead a long time."
How shall I answer that?

In what strange tongue,
Layered with dust?
Dust everywhere.

    (2012)

Roller Coaster Poem
_____

If I speak real fast, crosscut, flip, dissolve, divide, turn upside down at speeds exceeding 100 mph, crash head first into an exploding brick wall, wave my arms & scream like an idiot, will you understand what I am trying to say to you?

(2012)

The Contours Of Affection

Nothing about life I wish to forget.
Not the jazz of lifelong pain,
Nor the contours of affection
That make the days worth bearing.
I want to remember
The way a juggler remembers
The distance between his hands.
Someone must remember
The weight of love,
My wife's body beneath me,
Her mouth open,
Ageless floating outbursts,
Moon-legs &
The low sounds of sleep
Pouring into the night.
Everything on our travels
Speaks of mysteries.
All our lives: floating gardens.

(2008)

It's Not Just Dixie Anymore

The vocabulary of outlaws:
Before going to a hanging,
I can't master it fast enough.
All that Billy the Kid snarf,
Buckle, & horse fugue
(When you say that, stranger,
Smile!). Razzmatazz of
Grapeshot, & small eclairs
Of six-shooters clattering ecru
As the human spirit toughs
It out with its Colt 45,
That Peacemaker,
Looming large in the history
Of the 19th Century. Stuff
My saddlebags with live
Ammunition, then ride off
Into the sunset
With my Hole in the Wall Gang.
If big boy critics scoff,
Shoot 'em in the back.
It's one way to make peace.
Now in their spare time
The dead are whistling &
It's not just Dixie anymore.

(1989)

The Stain
_____

A mackerel sky: how stained is that?
I am the Prince of Stains,
The death of my 26 yr old son
Has stained me forever,
A stain so huge
It cannot be seen with the naked eye,
As my heart is stained
The way the night is stained
By fading starlight
It never asked for.

(2013)

Earthquakes
_____

Altho I have lost my son,
Life is still tolerable:
Sky is still the sky,
Wine is drinkable,

Friends come & go,
Love is bitter/sweet.
Earth holds steady
Under my feet.

Of course, earthquakes
Take their toll.
There are
Earthquakes still.

I no longer trust the earth
To bear my weight.

(2012)

Actually
———

I love the lightness of your
Fingers upon my body,
Slight upturn of your chin,
Small shadows everywhere
As we give into impulse
Followed by slight raise
Of your hips &
Inarguable touching,
Pale & painted & woven,
With so much fragrance,
All of you, actually.

(2004)

The Seasons

Winter's getting ready to drop
One more gut-bucket-honky-tonk cruel oil
On somebody's id.

Let roots freeze,
& the small crib of the moon
Hold delicate shadows

Of long ago sorrows.
I've got enough summer in me
To last a long time.

(2013)

How Many Lies Must I Tell To Protect Those I Love?

My son demands:
"Tell me why I shd go on living."
Put to the test
I guess I can come up with
Some false, some true reasons.
How many lies must I tell
To protect those I love?
The truth has sharp edges,
Is incomplete, cuts both ways.
I want you to go on living
Because you are my son.
We live for the sake of living.
I want you to want to go on living.

(2010)

Love Poem

The trout, according to Jeffries,
"Looks like a living arrow,
Formed to shoot through the water."

This summer
I have watched grown men
Wade for hours

In hope of achieving one.
Then when the trout,
With spots resembling

"Cachineal and gold dust,"
Had been "killed" then
Let go again,

An arrow thru water,
The unhooking of the barb,
This freeing

Into cold &
swirling mysteries vast,
I thought of my own long marriage,

Inborn with tiny breathings.

(2005)

The Map Of Human Reason

My God! These islands
Shimmer with discontent,
& are known for giants
Who kill with one blow,

Monsters with lantern jaws
Spout more false promises
Than local politicians.
Terra Incognita are everywhere.

The map of Reason
Has been redrawn many times.
How is it possible to tell
Valleys from the mountains.

Wander where you will,
Fields are mostly Monkshood
& Bushman Poison.
Barbarians under every rock.

The tallest pine trees
Cast no shadows.
Pause near their roots
& be strangled.

The strangest gods,
Ones with heads
Of crocodiles & hearts of stone
Are worshipped.

No wonder
So many of us hug
The rugged coastline.
& never go ashore.

    (2012)

The Island
―――――――

As the indifferent day
Swells to enormous size,
My world,
Crying "Hoy! Hoy!"
Is emptying out. Say

I have been hijacked,
Captured by pirates
On rough seas of love.
The Past
Is a mysterious island

Shrouded in fog.
When mariners land there,
Or any number
Of my darlings ,
To wander on the shore

Or among high wood,
Delving into caves.
Gathering
Driftwood, building fires,
They disappear forever.

    (2005)

The Map Of Human Reason 2

Mappa Causa with contour lines
Of wars gone awry,
Continents of thought confused &
Wary.

Cartographers work overtime
Measuring latitude
& longitude of synapse
Tides.

So many islands are treacherous,
Monsters at sea,
Barbarians under every rock,
Trees,

With roots in the air,
Cast no shadow.
No wonder most of us,
Knowing

What we know, fearing
The worse, sailing past
Many dangerous ports,
Thankful that our compass

Always points due North.

(2005)

Just How Confusing Is Spring?

No sense placing April on a pedestal,
When common wood-sorrel warbles
Lyrics by Dorothy Fields:
"It was not really Spring."
But, of course, it was really Spring.
What else cd it be?
That's how confusing Spring is.

    (2009)

Hustling Myself Out Of Existence

"Fifty years in the business and I'm still wearing a cardboard belt."
Zero Mostel in *The Producers*

Hustling myself out of existence,
Up & down deserted streets
I mean no one harm,
But shd like to wake just once
Not worrying about
 Filthy lucre. Dame Poverty greets

 Me with a leer. She's a queer
 Duck, queer as a 3 dollar bill.
 Don't have one of those either.
Gotta eat is her motto,
But I forget quite why,
My work shuffles wrong way
Down a one-way street. Sweet the liquor

Of forgetfulness, waters from Lethe
& other mystical tides.
Records spin, the melody is the same:
"Who will buy me a ticket to ride?"
The sum of all my life? I am loathe
To tell where Fame

& Fortune are hiding out,
Loathe to add up the income
& pay the tax,

Brackish with grimace, 50 yrs old
& still wearing a cardboard belt.
I need a thunderbolt, a jolt
From heaven to blaze me

From my Self. A sale?
Oh such small beer.

    (2007)

The Relentless Machinery Of Transport

Cursive this discourse:
I am running across a sodden field,
My gray striped pajamas
Falling to my knees.
I have been ordered to pull
The teeth of the dead,
Pitch gold & silver
Into Heaven's empty mouth,
Denounce my God,
Spit upon my loathsome self.
I roll about in a ditch,
My stomach distended by worms,

A cold wind blows from the East;
If I were a crow,
Feathers wd warm me.
If I were a fox,
Fur might protect me
From a sudden drop
In temperature,
But I am only human.
All I have to warm me are those I hate
& they run after me, smiling.

(2011)

The Structural Linguist Declares His Love To A Woman Named Cadence

Hark! My sweet,
No longer mock my context sensitivity,
For I must stride
Into your open structure
With prolongation.
Ah! My cognate, my Cadence,
Shall you ever know
How your distinctive acoustic features,
When blade &
Front of my tongue
Approach your alveolar ridge,
Swell paralanguages of desire?
Shall not your verb auxiliaries &
Mine ever intertwine?
Each night,
When your orality,
Brings upon me maximum stress,
I think upon of your muffling,
Your narrow nuclei,
Your internal close structures,
How swift my morphemes become unbound.
In short, my paradigm of mellowness,
It is imperative we take
The number 4 position
In the Four Position Syntax
Of Late Modern English,
Allowing your terminal contours
To swallow me in a semivowel glide.

Nay, my love, my sweet,
Stem not my fricative.

(2008)

"The Shining Wings On Which The Dragonfly Rides"

From the deck of my in-laws' country house I watch
A wet-meadow dragonfly of the genus *Sympetrum*.
How honest it is,
Taking only what it needs.
The sun means everything to it.
I myself have been lied to so many times
I wonder why I get up in the morning.
My younger 40 yr-old sister's phone has been disconnected,
So I have to call her at work.
She says We get older, we learn from experience,
But still we die stupid.
Wisdom, I suppose, meaning:
We don't trust one another
The way we used to.
So many human values, false values.
I tell her I find the phrase
WASTE NOT, WANT NOT abhorrent.
The rich have so much to waste &
They are not the ones in want,
While the poor, it is obvious,
Have nothing to waste.
Imagine dragonflies on the telephone:
"I'll meet you in the meadow at 10."
Even our wants turn out to be lies,
Even as I am, Dear Reader,
Lying to you now.
Does anyone care?
There they go: the dragonflies!
Black-faced skimmers, yellow wings.

For them, life must be so much more simple,
Their shadows nothing but a vein of wings.

(2010)

A Man And A Woman Enter The City Of Language To Articulate Their Desires

Whenever we enter this city,
I think of the line
Tai-hui wrote to Chen-ju Tao-jen:
"…words are the pointing finger,
Showing one where to locate the moon."
Well, I know where the moon is, &
I am certain you know where it is too.
So why do we need language
To articulate our desires?
Has not the Buddha warned us,
In so many words,
"Desire for what will not be attained
ends in frustration"?
Desire to speak true
Is so great a responsibility,
But the desire to remain silent
Is too great a burden to bear.
Do we not long for magic
To make the seasons kneel,
To make wind & forest walk downhill?
The City of Language,
Peopled as it is with anguish,
The kind of anguish,
That needs no explanation,
Is no place to live,
For whether we speak or no,
Planets go about their solitary businesses.
Listen! Rainmakers

Step from the pavilion,
Oracles with warnings in place of breath,
Thunder in their eyes &
Rainspur sprouting from their fingers.
Whenever we enter this city
I think of words, so many words.
One word and 10,000 beings spring into Being,
But once we forsake this city,
Where shall we go, &
How shall we ever know
When we have arrived there?

(2011)

Johnny Inkslinger Does The Black Bottom Stomp In Comicstrip Land And Rises Up Disappointed In America's Lack Of Values

---

Women have always been more interested in real life than I have been.
Real life is all right, but bogged down in errands, bills, & bad breath,
Tho even in comics strip land disappointments are rife:
No history there & sex performed fully clothed. Oh the troubles
I've seen!
Dagwood can't nap without some small boy knocking on his door;
death
Plays a mean clarinet, & all other characters trapped in panels,
Waiting (just like real life) for some gagster to put words in
their mouths.
Mary Worth dance with me just one more time,
Throw them child-bearing hips out, & pare Garfield down
To a couple of G strings. Oh, I'm going mad worrying about money,
Feeding the kids, paying the mortgage, running harder than ever.
Can't sit still. Oh stand up, Charle Brown, & be counted;
Uncle Spam Wants You! Solo me one more sixteen-measure theme,
For past participles of the American dream leave lots to be desired.
America, where is you? Pregnant with somebody's love child?
We are stomping in the Ozone Layer of Free Floating anxiety,
Sipping Dyspepsia Cola, shipping midnight bodies into
Heart Attack City,
(Comic book heroes too live on borrowed time; we get tired of them,
Discard them) wondering if Little Orphan Annie will ever get eyes
With real pupils in them, eyes to see the Truth with, tho not on TV,
Not in the comics, not in the movies. Sing it out loud, our
National Anthem:
The rich get richer, the poor get children. Up against Big Daddy

Warbucks,
Wall Street orgasms, Pentagon Blues, Siphoned-off-pension plans, etc.
We are all Sad Sacks. Brenda Starr, plant a big juicy one on my lips.
Why am I reading the comics? Oops. Sorry. Thought it was the
front pages.

(2008)

The Creation Of The Gentleman

> *"What fact more conspicuous in modern history than the creation of the gentleman?"* EMERSON

Most conspicuous in modern history,
At home in private clubs, competent at whist,
Devotee of the dry martini with a twist,
He never struck a woman -- with his fist.

(2010)

The World, It May Be Said

The world, it may be said,
Is divided into what exists
& what does not but could exist,
Measured by pain endured
Or not endured. Today a derelict

In blue jeans & a white T-shirt
Walking on Division Street
Bent down to pick up a cigarette
That had been flattened
On the sidewalk. Oh well,

Not all of us can sit around
& read & write poetry.
The incident reminded me of
A rodeo clown who said
His work was about as funny

As a funeral in the rain.

(2011)

On Reading The Encyclopedia Britannica From Cover To Cover

Do not know what to make of this fierce mountain of names.
Why do we climb it with so much stammering?
How is it possible to breathe in such thin oxygen,

When winds blister across the glaciers,
We seek shelters in hundreds of small huts, tho
How can we sleep when, under the rocks,

So many organisms, prolific with small dreaming,
Live & die, as I shall too, with ignorance & fears.
Often the wind chill factor is too intense, & snow

Falls. We have no choice: climb or die.
We plant flags on numerous plateaus,
Then turn back, descend to the real world,

Whatever the real world is, tho
After all is said and done, mountains will still be there.

(2010)

All Hell Breaks Loose At This Time Of The Year Once Again

> *"The passive voice is a curse"*
> *Ray Kytle's* Composition: Discovery And Communication

With the passive voice of Spring,
All Hell was broken loose.
Stupidified by bristling wind,
The world was split to blossom
With evasive buddings & Hah!
The bark and peel of landscape
Was tempted once again, *la la*, &
Made known, *la la*,
--As if a human gesture could be formed
From all such damp connivings.

(2009)

I Am The Errand Man

Lawrence of Spain's *Araba*.
I am the errand man.
Staggering into the bank:
"Dr. Livingston, I presume?"
Amid the local deli,
I bear messages to Garcia,
Laundry lists of experience,
Drop off notes to agon.
Filling hampers with bad dreams. On-
ward and sideways, Mon-
day thru Sun & moon
Day. Swift the messenger
To his appointed tasks
As I worship the icon
Of Unpaid Bills, light a can-
dle to swift deeds, con
Old widows out of rent mon-
ey, do what is necessary to survive.
Hey! This is living, right?
Drop off. Pick up. Move on.
Home I bring Existential bacon,
Ford the Nile of Pastrami.
Beowulf with a broken toaster,
Checks to sign, stamps to lick,
Envelopes to order, lines to stand in.
Aeneas ,with old cough drops on
His back, searching for his son.
Anything else for me to do?

(2007)

The Interpretation Of Dreams

The Earth Monster eats me alive.
First, right foot,
Then the left.
In the pounce of waking,
Nothing is left
But the rip, brood, &
Rapid descent of livelong
Inscribed with dreams yearning,
We have more gods
Than we know what to do with.
In the pulp of sleep
They totter in radiant tides
Of mornings, & evenings.
Our waking hours are rife
With immortals
Reminding us of resurrection,
That solitary language
No mortal speaks.
In the Abode of Warriors,
I have not fared well,
Have not been brave enough.
Something in my life
Has outrun my life,
But I dare not ask what it is.
I should have been more heroic,
Have trusted, or, at least, have slept
With the Plumed Serpent.
The Sacred in myself,
The Continuum, the Sacrifice,

Hail the Witness of our lives,
What we are between sleep & waking,
Between Coward & Fool.
Tell me what you dream &
I shall tell you what gods you worship.

    (2006)

Blues

How do you sing the Blues
If you don't have the Blues?
That's an age-old old question,

But why not just sing the Blues
Because you want to sing,
Say if some blue-gray morning

Wants to sit in your lap,
So you stand up
Just to let it go.

The Blues will arrive
On your doorstep, anyway,
Kick your dog,

Steal your motorcycle,
Ride off with your wife,
So you sing the

"There's not going to be
Too much you can do about it
Blues."

(2008)

Happiness

quoth the raven.
Flashbulbs *pop pop pop*
In Poe's pepperpot purple poem,
Micro-lives in turnaround.
The gods, craven
As usual, toss a sop

Of Happiness in forms
We rarely recognize.
Poe decides to revise
Happiness to *Nevermore!*
Happy choice! He awakes,
Rubs his eyes, blows his nose.

Suffering is none too subtle.
Indeed, entire nations
Have fallen on less,
Built on nothing more than this:
Fantastic terrors, Asian
Hordes, blood & gore --

False gods pressed
Like wilted lettuce
Against window lattice:
Corpses beyond measure,
Left unburied, uncovered.
"The kettle of pleasure

Bubbles over,"
Quoth the Raven in E-flat,
As if he wished to sing
Alas! Alas!
Upon a bust of Pallas:
    "If you believe that

I have a bridge I want to sell you."

    (2008)

A Rain Not Invented By Any Genius

Today is all rain &
All I can think about is how old I am getting,
A rain not invented by any genius,
That covers the countryside &
Every common being.
Even the interiors, the walls, are damp.

This afternoon, a young Japanese woman,
Whom we think mad,
Drags her electric keyboard
Into the open air.
She plays Bach to soothe our souls.
Long fingers of rain hit the keyboard &
Soft notes stir with tardy spirit.
The woman with her kerchief &
Fat legs is not mad.
We are the mad ones
Because we no longer wish,
In any weather, to be soothed.

(2010)

Truth Without Embellishment

The lst time my sons & I
Walked the hill to pick blueberries,
The grove was owned
By an old man I did not know.
He sat by the window,
Waiting for someone
To play chess with. His wife
Measured our berries
Into pint-sized baskets.
The 2nd time my sons & I
Walked up the hill,
The man's wife had died, &
The old man had sold his house
To his grandson & had moved
Into a trailer down the road.
But this year, the 3rd year,
The blueberries
Are more prolific
Than they have ever been.
We can't pick enough of them.

(1995)

Johnny Inkslinger Presumes To Cut In On Fred Astaire While He Is Dancing With Ginger Rogers

With flat feet & a far-away look in my eyes,
I have little sense of rhythm or of time,
Tho time weighs upon my shoulders
To a fare-thee-well.

Is that a violin playing
Or a petunia with petals of lead?
Ah the palpable feet!
External organs of locomotion
Gallanting all over the lot,
A sennight of gallumphing rhumba
cha-cha cavortte, obbligato.

Poetry has my two left feet on tap.
Ah! To whirl with unurgent grace,
Raise the metal mercury
A quarter inch or so,
Make my quietus with a bare bodice.

(2009)

No Matter What I Do

Sometimes in the heart of the old,
There is only foolish fire;
But I am not so old
That I cannot dance, nor so old
That I cannot love, tho
No matter what I do
God will have my guts for garters.

(2007)

Another Song Of The Cannibals

Once feeding on flakes that resembled confetti,
This dead goldfish is
Hardly worth bothering about really,
So let's not get overly sentimental,
Weep for Lycidas, And, o ye dolphins, etc.
What two-handed engine is at the door,
Trying to pump significance
Into a heart no bigger than a pin?
I didn't even bother to find out its sex,
Just a nameless creature in God's kingdom,
But he/she? brought no one any harm &
Did very little damage to the day,
Who, like most of us,
Never paused long enough to read
Anne Finch's (Countess of Winchilsea)
A Song of the Cannibals.

(2006)

Lacking The Courage To Be Happy

Lacking the courage to be happy,
I turn toward long lashes
Of light on the dunes
Where the sun achieves its measure of fame
Just by being there.

Day after relentless day.
We wander over the sand
As if standing outside is a vocation,
But what shall God say of me?
That I overstayed my welcome?
The hawk in the air, the dunes,
They are neither good nor bad,
But we, alas! are human &
Stammer out morals.

My eyes are opened,
But I do not always like what I see.
Is that such a sin?

(2012)

For That Summer When All The Wishing Went Out Of Me

Far into places
Where no person has been,
Even to the stay of stars
Not yet cancelled,
We carry our lives.
With cries, with kisses.
Our music all riffs,
We carry our lives
Like an arm
That has no hand at the end of it.

(2011)

My Mother The Allegory

What was she like
When my father first met her?
Today, nearing 80,
She is afraid to take
The down escalator.
No fear of going up, tho.

(1993)

Crude Night

Even in the best of times,
When the sun is shining &
I am free of pain.,
There is this sadness
That holds my life together.
What kind of sadness is it &
What is it doing to me?
Why have I gone so sour?
All these terrible things
That can happen.
I am writing to you
Against the backdrop
Of Interstellar war,
Fitful stages
Of gaseous debris,
But just because I have been taken over
By a telepathic alien,
Is that any reason for you
To turn away from me in disgust?

(2010)

Reading Action Comics 40 Years Too Late

Great Caesar's Ghost! 52 yrs old &
I am finally ploughing my way
Thru Clark Kent's secret identity.
I've had with it the cheesy foreflanks
Of Lit Crit. Literature is meant to fly,
Splatt! Whapp!
Time to spatter the streets of Metropolis
With finer tints of hemoglobin.
I tell you I was meant
To leap tall bildingromans
With a single bound, meant
To bend Lois Lane like steel
In my bare hands.
Time to stick dynamite
Up the ass of Shakespeare et. al.
Hamlet, with its cheap poisons,
Is not half so good as this.

(2005)

The Fury Of Sleet Under Streetlights

Everything falling
Out of heaven at once:
Airports closed; highways snarled.
Slush, mush, hail,
The order of the evening.

On nights like this
I identify wholly with Odysseus
Who just wanted to get home.
But the wine-dark sea
Is not my problem,
Nor the black-hulled ships.

My problem? The snow,
Coarse-grained & unrelenting,
Hurled into one's face, the fell
& fury of sleet under street lights.
The subways running late.
What disguise do I put on now?
What lies do I need to tell

To appease the nearsighted gods
Asleep in their own warm houses?

(2001)

Adolescence (2)

2 a.m. My 16 yr old son staggers home,
Slams the door, drops his coat.
"I don't care what you say," he says,
"I'm not listening."

   (2001)

Easter Sunday On The Basketball Courts

Two on two:
A certain meditative impulse is absent.
But I am too
Old for this, my whole Being bent
To Death & Resurrection, my lay-up skills
Shot to hell, my jump shot haywire.
Why do we kill each other?
Because there are not enough miracles,
Or because there are too many?
My sons & I had to
Sneak thru the chainlink fence
To reach this high court,
Not enough hoops in the city,
But there are enough guns.
Christ died for our sins,
But that has not stopped the traffic,
Easy, eccentric slaughter.
I am heavy with self-loathing, &
Lose control too easily.
My son rushes in for a lay-up,
An easy two.
He believes so much,
Whereas I believe so little.
The suffering of this world
Will not be redeemed
By Easter baskets or bunnies.
I am in a rage,

I take the ball, I fake,
I drive to the net. I miss.
It is not the end of the world.
Yet.

(1997)

Justice

In theory, the even-handedness of Justice
Is superior to all beauty. It scuttles
The atrociously wicked with a wave of a hand,
Allowing the innocent to walk freely & safely.

In theory, the wild landscapes of uncertainty
Are not its province, the dark ditches
Of despair. In theory, Justice is the custodian
Of all of God's best thoughts

But what Justice is there in this death
Where suffering is prolonged ,
When a tumor large as a hailstone
Keeps a woman from swallowing?

Virginia, you were never unkind
To any human being
As cancer was unkind to you.
Ah, but death is wonderful.

Now we can dirty the carpets &
Unmake the beds.
No one to scold me
For leaving coffee cups in the living room,

For not filling the dishwasher completely,
For buying too many lemons.
I think of your b&w television set,
The one with the poor reception,

The one with all the ghosts,
All that sex in the kitchen--
Discussions of abortions & cross-dressing,
Mid morning tittle-tattle

Of talk show piled upon talk show.
The tumbling gear
Of a new generation all on show
While one of Justice's golden scales

Dips lower than the other.

(1991)

How God Came To Me In Connecticut

You have to leave your house to find religion.
E.g, I was riding my bike
Down Sandy Beach road
When I looked up to see a nun on a motorcycle.
Rebel With A Cause, I guess,
Complete with black helmet
With a thick white cross painted on it.
The sand under my wheels went:
Te Deum, Te Deum, Te Deum.
She stopped to ask directions
From one who badly stammered,
Then off, burning rubber,
Gunning her life toward town.
I cannot tell you how my whole life lit up.

(2001)

The Tourniquet

I am just an old man
In an old man's body,
Grieving, bereft,

The world,
Tourniquet in hand,
Sits upon my chest
Turning, twisting, squeezing
Until I have no heart left.

(2011)

The Room
___

For friends the heart makes room
For comfort, nourishment, assuaging thirst;
But for one's sons or daughters,
That room was furnished from the first.

(2012)

April Broadcast

Nature is never wrong.
How cd she be?
At a farmhouse in Cologne,
Where St. Ursula &
11,000 virgins had been massacred,
An Emerson radio plays
A middle class comedy
By Carl Sternheim.
Across the meadow,
Alpine goldenrod
With its coarse toothed leaves
Bends low to hear:
"I touch the world.
& It breaks open."
Of course it does. It's spring.

(2011)

Nightwalker

Hazards of moonlight. I step
From the porch of sleep
Into night unending &
I walk thru it alone, up
The round rough, into
Sulk of momentary planets,
Return alone. When I awake
All the living & the dead
Are deep inside me.

(2012)

Who Would Live In A World Without Singing?

"*Sir*
Who wd live in a world without singing?
Listen! Black-crowned night herons
Turn their short thick necks
As the most casual tides with their run
Of catfish trill, *messa di voce*,
Mystery chords in balance & French Sixths
    on pungent wing.

As sun sets, unstreaked thrashers
Iterate phrases of lyric suites,
Madrigal comedies, intervals of
Varied thrushes holding fast
Throughout a fen of vibrato &
With contours of evening warming
    into myriad voices.

Who wd live in a world without singing?

(2010)

NEW POEMS

It Is 9 A.M. Do You Know Where Your Muse Is?

9 a.m Already I feel guilty
About not getting down to work,
Making the language jive &
Cash registers sing.
Why shd I get all hopped up
About sinking sweat
Into another day,
When the Universe has no need
For anything I do?
I am not exactly saving lives.

(2015)

Acceleration

Fast fast fast faster
Faster furious fast
Fast fast fast faster
Faster furious fast
Fast fast fast faster
Faster furious fast
Fast fast fast faster
Faster furious fast,
& you come upon
Something serious,
The glance of love
To slow you down.
Or a tragic thought,
Or great loss itself,
Which some knave
Might simply label
A speed bump…..

(2016)

Is Poetry Is A Ticket For Travel?

Poetry can transport you
From one dimension
Into another dimension,
From False to True

& back again. One more
Twilight Zone
To roast a hare in,
Whisking you from one place to another,

Faster than any Greyhound Bus.
A moment ago you were thinking
About sex,
 & now you are still thinking

About sex
But in a very different state.
Of course, Poetry
Cannot do everything.

(2016)

Aggiornamento

Swell. Now it's all right
For the sun,
Slipping sideways,
Revising day into night,
To speak Italian
To my foreign ears.

I bear the burden
Of the day,
But then who does not?
Time to revise my life,
Its nicks & dance
& subtle sway

Of loss. My wishes
Are rubbed
This way & that
Like small shells
Clicking In the hands
 Of children

 Not my own.

(2016)

Dawn In A Not So Classical Manner

& another thing:
She's too round-heeled,
Definitely involved
With too many people.
I'm merely the 5th wheel

On some erotic wagon
Going nowhere fast.
Agony, agony, agon,
Heat followed by frost.
Another 5 a.m. Yawn.

Then Rosy-nippled Dawn
Tossed one leg
Over the side of our bed,
Then the other,
Tossed on her robe of red

& fast as the speed of light
Raced out the door.
Waves of melancholy
Washed over
My thoroughly-used body.

Too early, I thought
To be saying Good-bye,
But, in this relationship,
She's the one
Who calls all the shots.

(2013)

Nothing Miraculous Here

The Self scolds itself,
It has nothing better to do.
Why can't I do better?
Something worthwhile,

Like Joshua --
Make the sun stand still.
My friend Josh
Died of brain cancer,

Radiation robbing him
Of his voice,
Desperation
In ordinary time

Hitting him
From every angle.
Nothing miraculous
There or here.

Grief
for a lost friend
Reveals
Another self.

(2015)

Absentee

Blue ice is one thing,
But I ain't walking on no bad ice,
The beautician sd. Unfortunately,
In the face of a breaking wind,
She stepped forth onto bad ice
& that was the last we heard of her
Until, many years later,
Her hometown voting center
Received an absentee ballot in her name.

(2016)

Thinking Of Wallace Stevens On The First Snowy Day In December

All right. So I swiped the title from Robert Bly.
Big fuckin' deal. Look what he did with it,
Dragging all over the place concierges
In gold clothes, virgins (whatever they are),
Skiffs under Greek clouds, beaches, waves –
What else have you got? Now look
What I'm going to do with the very same title.
Turn down the fictive music, please!
How shall I ever learn to think
With someone else's brain? Listen!
I am going to mention afternoon sleep,
Only to awake with Pale Women in Maryland
Where We Must Look For Help. Hell!
If I am going to steal one title,
I might as well help myself to the entire kit &
 caboodle

(2013)

Let's Say

Let's say you are half-way human
Sitting a local movie house.
In front of you there is a couple
Making out like bandits
& there is a wad of chewing gum
Stuck on the left arm of your chair.

You want to go outside to smoke,
But you don't. You remain
Stuck among images.
You watch for the 2nd or 3rd time
A scene where 2 soldiers
Meet in a movie theater.

Soon you realize that the theater
In the film is much nicer than the one
You are in. Still you don't walk out
Because there is nowhere else to go,
& because the love-making
In front of you is growing more intense.

You imagine his hand under her skirt,
& she ,of course, wears no panties,
So you decide to stay for the part
Where Robert Young
Describes the death of his grandfather,
Murdered in a bar,

Simply because he was Irish.

(2014)

Further Up The Track

An abandoned lot crammed
With abandoned trucks.
We are waiting for the train,
Bells ring, lights flash,
Candy-striped gates
Fall across the highway.
A deaf-man, dressed

In the American flag,
Carries more keys
Than the Janitor to Hell,
Wields his deafness
Like a baton, hits us
Over the head with it,
Wears a yellow button --
Girls rule --   then points
Toward the sign
That is his destination,
Not mine. Even
The large clock over
The Yellow Cab Co.
Is fifteen minutes fast.

Farther up the tracks,
A lumberyard
More organized
Than our local library.
On the waiting platform,
Counterfeiters
Are forging sunlight

For crows to scavange in.
Up & down the black tar
Mexican house cleaners,
Who cannot afford
To live in the town
In which they work,
Face a long commute.

Stand Back of the Yellow Line.

The train chugs in.
A chainlink fence
Divides one incoming track
From the outgoing one.
Passengers Dismount.
Others climb on.
This is life, we say.

This is life.

(2013)

Lover's Paradox

Say the heart's a glacier
Sliding south
Waiting to be warmed.
Say it is a hot coal
Always burning.
Both images can be true
At the same time.
No need to ask why.

(2014)

The Rehearsal

(for Ivan)

Earth, air, fire, water,
Then the 5th element: Music.
We showed our approval
After the Harpist's solo
By stamping our feet rapidly.
Scaling a huge mountain
Of solitude, onlookers stood,
Applauding, cheering,
While our conductor –
Who was, with so much joy
& waving of arms,
In his own element,
Motioned us on
To the next piece,
Deeper into Vivaldi's
"Concerto for Four Violins."
With a harpsichord on stage,
& the rehearsal clock
Ticking away,
We decided then & there,
All of us, musicians & audience,
We did not wish to die.

(2015)

The Leaping Place Of The Spirit

Ka tu ano tenei. O
When Death comes,
May it be cross-eyed!

At the Leaping Place of the Spirit,
I cd not help myself,
Overheard the brunette:
One evil night my uncle
Opened his door,
Someone tossed an egg,
The shell caught his eye &
My uncle scratched it;
It tore the cornea.
Today he's blind in one eye.
He looks normal,
But when he looks at you,
He looks a little cross-eyed.
I'm surprised he can drive.
I listened. I listened,
Then wandered outside
To chant a magic chant
to divert the rain.

(2013)

102° In The Shade

Fuck off, Sun
With your molten elements
& accelerating beamlines,
Enough is enough.
Wicked & cruel
This summer day
Perpetuating lithe bodies
In to *pas doble*
& other intricate steps.
All of Nature in heat,
Flaccid humors &
Multiple beeswax floatings,
Earth in a piss up
& birdsong in the lowlands,
Go away, go away.
Every extra breath
Is annoying
With all the evening stars
Laden with falling light
Gliding ever so slowly,
So slowly into port.

(2016)

One Down, 649,000 Hours To Go

*"Even a long human life adds up to
only about 650,000 hours."* Bill Bryson

The very first hour. O boy! O boy!
I haven't read *Madame Bovary*
Or *Lady Chatterley's Lover*
& have no intention to.

No Pop quizzes.
My mother's left breast
Is world enough for me.
Am I really as much me

As I am ever going to be?
& what about the doctor?
Why did he slap me?
I did nothing wrong.

When I grow larger,
I'm going to pay him
A little visit to give him
Something to remember me by.

649,000 more hours
To be the center of everyone's attention!
Wow! Let's get on with it.
Maybe I'll take up tap dancing.

(2016)

Sometimes

the title of a poem is so fine
The reader never reads another line.

(2014)

Yorick

I have jumped out of my skull.
What was my skull anyway
But a sidewinding planet
Of cat's eye constellations
Of what I was imagining
At any given instance,
Remnant thoughts
Such as the hugeness of love
Crowding out all other feelings.
Of course I have a mind
Filled with fitful reminiscences
Spinning in opposite directions
Like some dying star,
Galaxies of astonishments &
Gasps, high-speed shocks,
Odds & ends of theories,
Spirals of names & faces,
But what good will all this do me
In the Land of the Dead?

(2014)

Hamlet On The Tennis Courts

Benumbed by double faults,
The barometer
Of my emotional life
Hits an all-time low,
Storms on the horizon:
Six-Love, Six-Love, Six-Love.
Herein I set forth
Chronicles of my true shame,
Tho I know in my heart
The human heart
Is not necessarily kind,
Not necessarily anything worthwhile,
That often forgiveness
Is worse than condemnation.
My father dead. My first true love
Pushed around by her father.
Murder is never far from my thoughts.

The depravity of humankind,
Here, there & everywhere,
Spectators in lampshades
Made of human skin,
Applauding or hissing every shot.
What can they know
About my inner life,
Anatomies of my grief,
My disillusionments,
My lost beliefs?
I have missed so much.

Shall I be like Baudelaire &
Take six months
To make up my mind
To set forth or not
To the next village
Where I have seen starved children
Reduced to Edgar's diet,
"Mice and rats and such small deer"
Love-Six, Love-Six, Love-Six.

(2013)

Passing Thru The Landscape Will Not Help

Standing in a field
Of Dutchman's Breeches,
I think of Odysseus'
Escape from death.
(By the hairs of my nose,
I am growing older
As the randomness of life
Spills over me in earnest.)
How he boasted outside
The Cyclops' cave,
Calling out that he was No One.
As nightshine
Clusters & grinds
Over fields of April round,
The coming Indian Turnip,
Ghostflowers & twisted stalks,
I pretend to be myself,
Usually treated as no one,
Escaping from nothing,
Not even the work
Of fashioning ways
To describe ourselves
To ourselves.
As Sartre wrote to Beauvoir:
"I am not bored,
But I cannot figure why."
Passing thru the landscape
Does not help.

(2013)

Worry

Who has been a more faithful wife to me than Worry?
Spalled from the finest house of Heaven,
The Goddess of Dawn sits propped at my window:
Peering in, she asks: "Who is that sassy broad
Shaking her platinum braids
All over your elbows? Why do you insist
On snuggling into every cavity of her being?
Has she not stuffed your face with sweetbreads of despair?"
Tossing and turning, my faint life answers:
Who has been a more faithful wife to me than Worry?
Has she not slept with me every night of my life?

(2013)

From One Great Perhaps To Another

Standing in the Bank of Bad Debts, I ask:
What is spiritual reality to me?
Someday I am going to explode.
Late Thursday afternoon
In the middle of my life,
I grow larger & larger.
The outward ease of being one's self,
What a farce it all is,
Another day linked to loss.
Fraught with the usual perils,
I scurry from one Great Perhaps to another,
Sketching moustaches
On the face of Mortality
With its undiscovered laws,
Its endless search engines
For songs yet unrecorded.
This is how I pay my debts:
I sing for my supper.

(2013)

The Narrows Of Another Life

In the narrows of another life
Wind-cooled moonlight
Above the thistle dimmed,
The gadwell's *bek* & hue
Whistle down the tide
Where many a breathing thing
To my sleeping side
Purses its mouth, whispering
Me over the precipice
Into dreams where my 1st love,
White-gowned, kisses.
She speaks, urging me to live,
All about me the bulk of song:
Live, live, live,
No finger to her lips: Shhh!

(2013)

Falling Asleep On The Train To Boston

Dead leaves in my head
& a hint of ammonia
In the autumn air
With the Concord Squad rattling,
But what do we get in return
When we surrender our youth?
On the outskirts of Watertown,
The conductor appeared.
The solid sound of the ticket punch.
I asked what he knew
About Morpheus & Hypnos,
& other slow sons of sleep?
He replied: They have to have
A ticket to ride. A ticket
To ride. A ticket to ride,
Ride, ride. A ticket. *Click*.
Click punch click. Ticket
Just like everybody else.

(2015)

May We Talk About Something Else?

Yes, I know you want to get laid,
But may we talk
About something else,
Not the usual sexual squeak & squawk.
What about the oceans of the world?
Oceans are so stupid;
Not one has an I.Q. over zero
& often their tides are ripped
For splendid drownings. A musician
In 1960s San Francisco,
Gazing at that wet vastness of Pacific,
Sighed. "Far out! That ocean is no
Friend of Man. It harbors creatures
No sane person
Wd invite home for supper." Far out.
Indeed it is & conditions worsen
As the heavens heave & the tide
Stutter & stalls.
For eons, oceans have butted heads
Against shore-lines & sea-walls,
Until the seas have no brains left.

(2016)

Ruins

Darius Rucker is singing:
Rock me momma like a wagon wheel,
But I'm not listening
All that closely. I am thinking
Of Largo Argentina in Rome,
How it is possible to stand
Anywhere in the world,
In foreign lands or at home
To contemplate History,
Ancient worlds in ruin.
Wind across the poplars,
Patter of soft rain,
Each seems to cry
"Why must our statesmen
Send so many of us
Off to lying wars to die?"
Rock me momma like a wagon wheel.

(2016)

There Is Always A Ship Sailing Somewhere Over Crazy Weeds

Lifting up the skirts
Of the cheerfully invisible.
My life is never so bad
As I make it seem.
It is, however, a mess,
Un bordel of unpaid bills,
Gods grinding & grinding,
Making mash of my days.

Of course, there is the sense
That someone is missing.
Every day someone vanishes,
900 immigrants
Falling off a boat, capsizing,
Drowning. But what's the sense
In holding back?
There is always a ship sailing

Somewhere over crazy weeds.
Wind takes the sails & we go.
Few persons insist that Life,
Textured with yearnings,
Has to last so many yrs
Or that we must forgive
All the cruelties laid upon us.
Each day contains some act
That will not be tidy.

(2015)

Whistling Past The Graveyard In The Better Part Of Town

Am I alive or dead?
Do not be hasty. Take your time.
The answer may not be obvious.
I am like a young child
Whistling past the graveyard.
A north wind rattles the gates,
The padlock is rusted.
The company that owns
This vast acreage
 Does not make it easy to get into.
 Every time the Earth is opened up
& a coffin is lowered,
Grave voices whisper:
Location, location, location.

(2015)

Pleasures

How much thought did I give
To my parents' pleasures?
Their Saturday nights out,
Or late summer afternoons
With a few holes of golf?

What pleasures they took
In the forbidden world at large
Or in their small bedroom
Near our one bathroom

Where the tiles were cracked
& the bathtub stained yellow.
How often the house strained
To contain frayed affections,

Money worries, ulcer flare-ups,
My grandmother's bronchitis.
Their hearts formed my heart too.
Why didn't I pay more attention?

(2016)

For My Lost Son

They say nothing lasts forever,
But even if that were so
Please do not think I am indifferent
To the stillness that grows
In all of us. What I might not do,
Amid the richness of the world,
Is stay forever.
Even Love cannot hold me.

I touch the wind & its web
& they touch back. What I might not do
Is to walk away singing.
Farther away in the world
Is another world
Where I repeat your name
Over & over.

(2014)

Saturday Morning In The Laundry Room

While I deal with the All, sorry
Stains of my life deepen, & my thoughts
Rise & fall in a tumble, &
Pygmy armies are put to flight.

O why I am not waltzing
In bloody Transylvania hot spots,
Or digging pits
For Mastadons? or building huts

On the edge of some savage country,
Where I cd be a philosopher-prince?
But no, I am stuck with Brite,
Doing my starch-legged dance

On the Rialto of Rinse.

(2013)

Is This What We Have Lived For?

Enter forlorn, four lorn sailors
Sailing the 7 seizures

Of a world sized & seized,
Land seizures, soul seizures.

Flourish of Cornets
With every other star in the sky vibrating,

Luxurious light on hold,
Dark stars on holiday.

Is this what we have lived for?
The end of things?

Out of what fire,
Shall we burn off all our losses?

(2014)

American Haiku: The Lie Detector

There are only five words in this line.
2 words here,
& no words in this one.

(2015)

You Could Be Wrong

The ocean of bad dreams
(You certainly do not need
Latitude & longitude
To locate that immensity, do you?)
"Inmantled in ambrosial dark"
As Tennyson might say & did.
Well, there you are,
Standing or swimming,
Deliciously cold,
Amid large sheaves of
Rising & falling,
When suddenly you are surrounded
By more than 100 Hammerhead sharks.
When your blood goes chill,
You believe you have no further need of poetry.
You cd be wrong.

(2013)

Annual Report From The Planet Money

Money, here in the Nebula of Want, is
The far-away planet
Everybody lives upon or
Wants to live upon. When I was
Younger,
I cd write home for $$$$$$$$$$, &
My letters wd be answered,
But today I am my own house,
Where Mail arrives 3 weeks too late.
How imaginative I am
Awaiting Eternity of Cold Cash,
Ducking ultra-dense fiscal shrapnel.
Too many years have passed.
Rain falls harder now, & what was to be
Has not been,
Starcrunch mutterings
Upon supernovas of missed opportunities,
Within the Roche limit of 3
Planetary radii of a Million Big Ones,
Debts pulse violently.
What intense surface pressures exert
Dead Weight
Upon this knobby region
Where the mean velocity of
Annual Income is
5.0222 km/second. Thus,
I hold on for dear life.
In such thin atmosphere

(2013)

Trouble 101

All right, class. Listen up.
Lieber & Stoller
Wrote *You looking for trouble*,
Elvis sang the words,
& we, gyrating our hips,
Sang back. Take notes.
Crawfish Hannah is absent,
She took her troubles
Down to Madam Ruth,
But if the rest of you punks
Are looking for trouble,
No need to place an ad
In the Penny Gazette,
Nor sign up
For Instant Gratification
Dating Services,
Nor even step outside.
We got trouble right here
In River City.
Most drop-outs already know,
But few admit it,
Not even to themselves,
That when you decide
To look for trouble,
You've already found it.

(2016)

Just Another Spring Poem

O.K. O.K. K.O. Winter
By adding one more
Yaddi ya yaddi ya
Hip hop & whistle
Subatomic verse
To immense stockpiles
Of ring-a-ding-ding
Hail to blithe Spring
Resurrections.

More rain coursing
Thru the mud fields,
Fragrant winds
Across star thistle,
While every shore
& branch bristles
With unfettered wooing,
Not for the faint of heart
In & out, up & down,
Poke-a-poke mating
Sex in bushes,
Under tree stumps
& a codependent moon,
Moist kingdoms all aglow,
More than half buzz,
Buzz, burr & stir
& hum invisible
to the naked eye.
That sort of thing.

    (2014)

The Obligatory Scene

It is appropriate
That the switchblade appears here
Because it will be used later
When we cut open readers' hearts
Just for the sheer

Joy of it, slice through
Organs of increase with enormities
Of hurt, slicing Envy
Into bite-size squares.
All this blood to tease

Out genuine feeling,
A line or two of praise,
Until we walk out onto the roadway,
Smiling, greeting strangers
With "Have a nice day!"

    (2015)

All Back Story

18 1/2 ounces or a pound of clever. But
What does that have to do with Truth?
As for "Higher Truths"-- which Truth is higher?
2 x 2 = 4. Or that there are black holes
Emitting musical tones? You might ask
Why doesn't Hollywood produce a movie
Where Cary Grant plays the universe,
Snow White & 7 Dwarf Planets.
Alas! The Universe is all back story.
Later the moon comes into play.

(2013)

"Fortune That Arrant Whore"

Just to speak her name
Stirred pleasant fantasies,
So in a black skirt
Shorter than this verse.
She asked: "Want a good time?"

Of course. Who doesn't?
But when she quoted
Her price
I demurred. It was too high,
So Fortune

Turned her back to me,
& walked away.
I have called her name
More than once
Have begged for her to return.

She does not
Even bother to reply.

(2016)

Even Sleep Takes Us

Breathing, consciousness, memory:
It is difficult to take leave of
The only worlds we know

Our bodies too are blossoms,
All those strange stirrings,
The upwardness

Of events glimpsed
Then forgotten. At day's end,
The grace of the world

Descends upon us
As we settle into sleep.
Even sleep takes us upward.

(2014)

Oh God! Not Another Poem About Hope!

Somewhere along the line (alexandrine)
Some makeshift I-Get-No- Respect poet
Will tackle the theme of Hope,
Imitating, perhaps, the very verse
Moliere's Alceste despised so much.
Of course any I-don't- read-no-dopey-
Poetry person who reaches
Beyond his or her teens realizes
The best poem on Hope is but a single line
Penned by Benjamin Franklin
In his *Poor Richard's Almanac*:
"He that lives upon Hope, dies farting."

(2013)

Field Guide To Wild Flowers

The world comes at me
From so many different directions
My sadness falls all over itself.
The central work of my life is
To hold my life together,
To stand in wonder
Before the sudden course
Of Nature, by sky & soil,
Solomon's Seal, Mountain Bellwort,
Gall-Of-The-Earth, as if my soul
Should be enfolded by
The spin of most distant stars,
Rippling tides of suns
& furious wine-dark oceans
Holding in their wash
Centuries of animals alive & dead.

(1916)

ACKNOWLEDGEMENTS

"Standing at a Gate in Summer" appeared originally in *South Dakota Review* (Spring, 1972)

"Reflections From La Mancha" appeared originally in *Fragments* (Winter 1969).

"To Those Who Wronged Me, Most Unjustly So," appeared originally in *Poetry Florida And*, II (Fall;, 1968)

"Monopoly" appeared originally in *Epoch* (Winter, 1971)

"To One Who Suffered a Miscarriage in London" appeared originally in *New England Review* (Spring, 1972)

"A Dance For Big Bad John" appeared originally in *Florida Quarterly*, VI (July, 1976)

"Ordinary Cities" appeared originally in *Spirit: A Magazine of' Poetry* (Spring-Summer 1979-80)

"My Milching Malicho" appeared originally in *The Nebraska Review*, XIII (Winter, 1984)

"Yorick" appeared originally in *Allegro Poetry Magazine* (September 2016).

"It Escapes Me" appeared originally in *Southern Poetry Review*, 45 (2007)

"*On Reading The Man in the Gray Flannel Suit* Some 35 Years After Publication" appeared originally in *Northwest Review* (November 2011)

"In the Narrows of Another Life," "Falling Asleep on the Train to Boston," and "Ruin appeared originally in *Offcourse #66.*

"There is Always a Ship sailing somewhere over Crazy Weeds," "Whistling Past the Graveyard in the Better Part of Town," and "Saturday Morning in the Laundry Room" appeared originally in *Offcourse* #64.

* * *

The most important acknowledgements are saved for Jack Estes, my friend and publisher whose editing and proof-reading went far beyond the call of duty, for Laura Tolkow who has designed all my Pleasure Boat Studio books, and for all those editors of literary publications who have published my poems and have encouraged my work, such as it is.

ABOUT THE AUTHOR

Louis Phillips was born in 1942 in Lowell, Massachusetts, but when he was eight years old his parents, two younger sisters, and his grandmother moved to Hollywood, Florida. In l964, he graduated from Stetson University. He then earned an M.A. in Radio, Television, and Motion Pictures from the University of North Carolina at Chapel Hill. He earned a second M.A. in English and Comparative Literature from the City University of New York. Since then he has taught English, film studies, & humanities at several colleges and has published more than fifty books for children and adults. His sequence of poems –The Time, The Hour, The Solitariness of the Place –was the co-winner in the Swallow's Tale Press competition (1984). Among his published books of poems are The Krazy Kat Rag (Light Reprint Press), Bulkington (Hollow Spring Press), The Time, The Hour, The Solitariness of the Place (Swallow's Tale Press). His short story collections include A Dream of Countries Where No One Dare Live (SMU Press), Bus to the Moon (Fort Schuyler Press), The Woman Who Wrote 'King Lear' (Pleasure Boat Studio), Must I Weep for the Dancing Bear? (Pleasure Boat Studio), and Galahad in the City of Tigers (World Audience). Broadway Plays Press published three of his full-length plays: The Last of the Marx Brothers' Writers, The Envoi Messages, and The Ballroom in St. Patrick's Cathedral Four collections of his one-act plays are available at Amazon.com. He teaches at the School of Visual Arts in NYC.

Books from Pleasure Boat Studio: A Literary Press:

Listed chronologically by release date:

Poems from Ish River Country • Robert Sund • $16
Tom Hall & the Captain of All These Men of Death • Russell Hill • $17
Headwaters: Poems and Field Notes • Saul Weisberg • $17
House of Burnt Offerings • Judith Skillman • $16
The Juried Heart • James Clarke • $17
The Whiskey Epiphanies • Dick Bakken • $17
For My Father • Amira Thoron • $17
Return to a Place Like Seeing • John Palmer • $17
Ascendance • Tim McNulty • $16
Alter Mundus • Lucia Gizzino • trans. from Italian by Michael Daley • $15.95
The Every Day • Sarah Plimpton • $15.95
A Taste • Morty Schiff • $15.95
Dark Square • Peter Marcus • $14.95
Notes from Disappearing Lake • Robert Sund • $15
Taos Mountain • Paintings and poetry • Robert Sund • $45 (hardback only)
A Path to the Sea • Liliana Ursu, trans. from Romanian by Adam J. Sorkin and Tess Gallagher • $15.95
Songs from a Yahi Bow: Poems about Ishi • Yusef Komanyakaa, Mike O'Connor, Scott Ezell • $13.95
Beautiful Passing Lives • Edward Harkness • $15
Immortality • Mike O'Connor • $16
Painting Brooklyn • Paintings by Nina Talbot, Poetry by Esther Cohen • $20
Ghost Farm • Pamela Stewart • $13
Unknown Places • Peter Kantor, trans. from Hungarian by Michael Blumenthal • $14
Moonlight in the Redemptive Forest • Michael Daley • includes a CD • $16
Jew's Harp • Walter Hess • $14
The Light on Our Faces • Lee Whitman-Raymond • $13
God Is a Tree, and Other Middle-Age Prayers • Esther Cohen • $10
Home & Away: The Old Town Poems • Kevin Miller • $15

Against Romance • Michael Blumenthal • $14
Days We Would Rather Know • Michael Blumenthal • $14
Craving Water • Mary Lou Sanelli • $15
When the Tiger Weeps • Mike O'Connor • with prose • 15
Concentricity • Sheila E. Murphy • $13.95
The Immigrant's Table • Mary Lou Sanelli • with recipes • $14
Women in the Garden • Mary Lou Sanelli • $14
Saying the Necessary • Edward Harkness • $14
Nature Lovers • Charles Potts • $10
The Politics of My Heart • William Slaughter • $13
The Rape Poems • Frances Driscoll • $13

The following books are from Empty Bowl Press, a Division of Pleasure Boat Studio:

Hanoi Rhapsodies • Scott Ezell • $10
P'u Ming's Oxherding Pictures & Verses • trans. from Chinese by Red Pine • $15
Swimming the Colorado • Denise Banker • $16
Lessons Learned • Finn Wilcox • $10
Petroglyph Americana • Scott Ezell • $15
Old Tale Road • Andrew Schelling • $15
Working the Woods, Working the Sea • Eds. Finn Wilcox, Jerry Gorsline • $22
The Blossoms Are Ghosts at the Wedding • Tom Jay • with essays • $15
Desire • Jody Aliesan • $14
Dreams of the Hand • Susan Goldwitz • $14
The Basin: Poems from a Chinese Province • Mike O'Connor • $10 / $20 (paper/ hardbound)
The Straits • Michael Daley • $10
In Our Hearts and Minds: The Northwest and Central America • Ed. Michael Daley • $12
The Rainshadow • Mike O'Connor • $16

Untold Stories • William Slaughter • $10 / $20 (paper / hardbound)

Our Chapbook Series:

No. 1: *The Handful of Seeds: Three and a Half Essays* • Andrew Schelling • $7 • nonfiction
No. 2: *Original Sin* • Michael Daley • $8
No. 3: *Too Small to Hold You* • Kate Reavey • $8
No. 4: *The Light on Our Faces* – re-issued in non-chapbook (see above list)
No. 5: *Eye* • William Bridges • $8
No   6: *Selected New Poems of Rainer Maria Rilke* • trans. fm German by Alice Derry • $10
No. 7: *Through High Still Air: A Season at Sourdough Mountain* • Tim McNulty • $9 • with prose
No. 8: *Sight Progress* • Zhang Er, trans. fm Chinese by Rachel Levitsky • $9 • prosepoems
No. 9: *The Perfect Hour* • Blas Falconer • $9
No. 10: *Fervor* • Zaedryn Meade • $10
No. 11: *Some Ducks* • Tim McNulty • $10
No. 12: *Late August* • Barbara Brackney • $10
No. 13: *The Right to Live Poetically* • Emily Haines • $9

From other publishers (in limited editions):

In Blue Mountain Dusk • Tim McNulty • $12.95 • a Broken Moon Press book
China Basin • Clemens Starck • $13.95 • a Story Line Press book
Journeyman's Wages • Clemens Starck • $10.95 • a Story Line Press book

Orders: Pleasure Boat Studio books are available by order from your bookstore, directly from our website, or through the following:

SPD (Small Press Distribution) Tel. 8008697553, Fax 5105240852
Partners/West Tel. 4252278486, Fax 4252042448
Baker & Taylor 8007751100, Fax 8007757480
Ingram Tel 6157935000, Fax 6152875429
Amazon.com or Barnesandnoble.com

Pleasure Boat Studio: A Literary Press
201 West 89th Street
New York, NY 10024
www.pleasureboatstudio.com / pleasboat@nyc.rr.com

www.ingramcontent.com/pod-product-compliance
Lightning Source LLC
Chambersburg PA
CBHW052020290426
44112CB00014B/2309